All Hail the Power of Jesus' Name

Diadem

JAMES ELLOR
Arranged by Robert MacDonald

1

2

Abide with Me

Eventide

WILLIAM HENRY MONK
Arranged by Robert MacDonald

Add 32'

All Glory, Laud, and Honor

St. Theodulph

MELCHIOR TESCHNER
Arranged by Robert MacDonald

All Glory, Laud, and Honor— 2

Away in a Manger

Mueller

JAMES R. MURRAY
Arranged by Robert MacDonald

Break Thou the Bread of Life

Bread of Life

WILLIAM F. SHERWIN
Arranged by Robert MacDonald

PIANO

ORGAN

Gt.

© Copyright 2001 Broadman Press (SESAC) in *Fairest Lord Jesus*.
Nashville, TN 37234.

Crown Him with Many Crowns

Diademata

GEORGE J. ELVEY
Arranged by Robert MacDonald

Fairest Lord Jesus

Crusaders' Hymn (St. Elizabeth)

Schlesische Volkslieder, 1842
Arranged by Robert MacDonald

Great Is Thy Faithfulness

Faithfulness

WILLIAM N. RUNYAN
Arranged by Robert MacDonald

Great Is Thy Faithfulness — 2

Hark! The Herald Angels Sing

Mendelssohn

FELIX MENDELSSOHN
Arranged by Robert MacDonald

PIANO

ORGAN

Gt.

Hark! The Herald Angels Sing— 2

Hark! The Herald Angels Sing— 4

Holy, Holy, Holy
Nicaea

JOHN B. DYKES
Arranged by Robert MacDonald

Holy, Holy, Holy — 3

Hosanna, Loud Hosanna

Ellacombe

Gesangbuch Wittenberg, 1784
Arranged by Robert MacDonald

Hosanna, Loud Hosanna — 2

Joy to the World! The Lord Is Come

Antioch

GEORGE FREDERICK HANDEL
Arranged by Robert MacDonald

Joy to the World! The Lord Is Come — 2

Morning Has Broken

Bunessan

Traditional Gaelic Melody
Arranged by Robert MacDonald

Morning Has Broken — 2

O Come, O Come, Emmanuel

Veni Emmanuel

Plainsong;
adapted by THOMAS HELMORE
Arranged by Robert MacDonald

O Come, O Come, Emmanuel — 2

36

O Come, O Come, Emmanuel — 3

Spirit of God, Descend upon My Heart
Morecambe

FREDERICK C. ATKINSON
Arranged by Robert MacDonald

Spirit of God, Descend upon My Heart — 2

Spirit of God, Descend upon My Heart — 4

The First Nowell

The First Nowell

Traditional English Carol
Arranged by Robert MacDonald

The First Nowell — 2

The First Nowell — 4

This Is My Father's World
Terra Patris

FRANKLIN L. SHEPPARD
Arranged by Robert MacDonald

This Is My Father's World — 3

What Child Is This

Greensleeves

Traditional English Melody
Arranged by Robert MacDonald

What Child Is This — 2

What Child Is This — 4

When I Survey the Wondrous Cross

Hamburg

LOWELL MASON
Arranged by Robert MacDonald

Worthy of Worship

Judson

MARK BLANKENSHIP
Arranged by Robert MacDonald